THE PONIES

BY
NANCY ROBISON

EDITED BY
DR. HOWARD SCHROEDER
Professor In Reading and Language Arts
Dept. of Elementary Education
Mankato State University

DESIGNED & PRODUCED BY
BAKER STREET PRODUCTIONS
MANKATO, MINNESOTA

COVER GRAPHICS BY
BOB WILLIAMS

CRESTWOOD HOUSE
Mankato, Minnesota

LIBRARY OF CONGRESS CATALOGING IN PUBLICATION DATA

Robison, Nancy.
  The ponies.

(Horses, pasture to paddock)
SUMMARY: Discusses the many types of ponies and how to buy and care for them.
  1. Ponies--Juvenile literature (1. Ponies.) I. Schroeder, Howard. II. Title. III. Series.
SF325.R6   1983   636.1'6   83-7833
ISBN 0-89686-229-1

International Standard Book Numbers:	Library of Congress Catalog Card Number:
Library Binding 0-89686-229-1	83-7833

PHOTOGRAPH CREDITS

Sharyn Fellenz/Pony of the Americas Club: Cover, 20, 45
Alix Coleman: 4, 13, 28, 43
Patti Mack: 8, 27
Cappy Jackson: 9, 31
United Press International: 10, 23, 38
Joseph Berke/Hammitt's Belgians: 15, 17, 32, 34, 40, 42
Pony of the Americas Club: 21
Curtis J. Badger: 22
Cindy McIntyre: 24
Pennington Galleries: 25
Jackie Zellmer: 39

CRESTWOOD HOUSE

Hwy. 66 South, Box 3427
Mankato, MN 56002-3427

TABLE
OF
CONTENTS

Ponies are just the right size for children.

INTRODUCTION

Ponies are not newborn or young horses. Nor is a pony just a small horse. Ponies are a separate breed, or type, of horse. A pony may be as small as twenty inches (51 cm), but no larger than fifty inches (128 cm). They are the right size for children and some small adults to ride. Ponies can give young riders the confidence to eventually ride full-sized horses.

To understand the pony it is helpful to know its background.

① HISTORY OF PONIES

Thousands of years ago, small horses roamed the earth. They were only twelve inches (31 cm) high, and had four toes on their front feet and three on their back feet. They had short necks and tails, and their manes were of short, stiff hairs. These horses were called *Eohippus,* or Dawn Horse.

The Dawn Horse ate only tender leaves. Its teeth were not strong enough for anything else. Dawn Horse became a fast runner to escape its enemies. It later developed hoofs with which it could kick the enemies it couldn't outrun. Running and kicking are still strong traits in today's ponies.

Dawn Horse also had to develop good eyesight for spotting enemies at a distance. Its close-up eyesight, however, did not develop as well. Today's pony must look very closely at any obstacle in its path; otherwise the pony might trip over it.

A pony's sharp sense of smell and hearing, also passed on to it from its ancestors, may cause it to react to something the rider does not see or hear. This reaction often causes the rider to think that the pony was "spooked."

During the many years that Dawn Horse was developing all these characteristics, other parts of its body changed, too. Its mane and tail got thicker, and it began to weigh more. The horse could eat tougher grass as its teeth became stronger. And it got a new name — *Mesohippus,* or in-between horse.

Because of the horse's development, or changes, it has survived to modern times while other prehistoric species, such as dinosaurs have died out. When Columbus discovered America, there were no horses here. The Spanish brought ponies to Mexico and the western United States in the early sixteenth century. Some of these ponies ran away and hid in the mountains. They became the wild herds of mustangs that are still around today.

Indians captured some of the wild horses and learned to ride them. Settlers caught others and used them for farm work and for pulling wagons. All of

American Indians learned how to ride the mustangs.

these horses were ponies, not full-sized horses as the movies show them.

Early North American settlers also brought ponies with them from England. A tough, steady pony was the best animal they could bring. Besides taking up little room, the pony did not eat much. And it could do almost the same work as a full-sized horse.

As America grew, so did the use of the horse. Bigger, stronger horses were needed to pull bigger wagons and to do heavier work.

People began to breed ponies for different tasks. From this breeding the Morgan horse was developed. It was a good riding horse and a good harness horse. It could run, trot, pull and outwork every other horse around. From the Morgan horse came

The Morgan horse was developed to do many things.

the carriage horse and the trotters. Some of the Morgan horses' bloodline is in every Saddle Horse, Tennessee Walker and Quarter Horse. All of these horses came from a little pony that a man named Justin Morgan raised.

In 1820, ponies began to appear at fairs and shows. Most of these ponies came from the Shetland Islands near Great Britain. They became so popular that the American Shetland Pony Club was formed in 1888.

The pony was used to pull buckboards and small wagons. And ponies were used by many children until the day the bicycle arrived. The pony became even less important after the automobile and tractor arrived in the early 1900's. Then came the depression of the 1930's. People no longer could afford to keep a pony just for the fun of it. Ponies almost disappeared.

Today, however, the pony world is bigger than ever before.

This pony is being used to pull a peddler's wagon.

② TYPES OF PONIES SHETLAND

Of the many types of ponies, the most famous and widely used is the Shetland. It is the smallest of all

In England, a little girl rides her Shetland pony next to a full-sized horse.

pony breeds and is the most popular. The Shetland gets its name from its homeland — the Shetland Islands. They are located fifty miles (80.6 km) north of Scotland and three hundred and fifty miles below the Arctic Circle. There are no trees on these islands and only strong, healthy animals can live there.

Norsemen from Scandinavian lands brought horses to the Shetland Islands more than two thousand years ago. These Vikings carried the horses with them on their "long ships." The horses had to be small or they wouldn't have fit in the ships. The land was cold and there wasn't much to eat. With only salt marsh grasses, heather, and kelp from the sea, the horses became even smaller. But the pony also grew strong. It could take care of itself.

Early Shetland ponies, sometimes called "Shelties," were chunky and heavy boned. They had shaggy coats. Many, many years later, when they came to America, they were changed.

Through selective breeding they had become more pleasing to the eye. No changes were made in the height of the pony. But today, the legs of the Shetland are longer. The Shetland's forehead is wider, and the eyes are more alert. The pony has well-formed nostrils and small ears that are pointed. It has a full mane and tail. The neck is thin and long and flows gracefully into the gentle shape of the pony's body.

The American Shetland is divided into two

groups. The "over" and the "under." This refers to over forty-three inches or under forty-three inches (110 cm). The "under" group is the most popular. A Shetland pony can be as short as thirty-six inches (92 cm) or as tall as forty-six inches (117 cm) and it can weigh from two hundred to five hundred pounds (91-227 kg).

Both types are known for their sure-footedness. Like goats, they can walk almost anywhere. They have strong legs. But better than anything, they have patience and intelligence.

Shetlands were imported to the United States as children's pets. When horse breeders decided that a larger, flashier pony would be more popular, they bred the Shetland to the large Hackney pony. Many of today's Shetlands have so much Hackney blood that they no longer are a good size for small children to ride. But these crossbred ponies have slender legs, delicate heads, and silken manes and tails. These characteristics make them popular show animals.

In addition to being used for riding and showing, ponies have been good work horses.

There is a famous story about Bressy, a brave little pony that worked in a coal mine many years ago. When the coal mine became flooded, ten miners were trapped. Bressy swam through the dark waters. She came back with one miner hanging onto her tail. Then went back and got a second miner. On her third trip, she came back with one miner holding her tail and the rest of them swimming behind. She had shown them the way out. Is it any wonder that she became the pet of those miners? For the rest of her life, she lived in comfort in a nice pasture.

THE HACKNEY PONY

The Hackney pony is called the Prince of Ponies. It is a real show pony that loves to prance and show

The Hackney pony loves to show off.

off. The Hackney originally came from England.

The Hackney pony is a harness pony only. That is, it is not saddled and ridden. It is used to pull a viceroy (a four-wheeled, light carriage). This pony rarely walks or gallops. It has two gaits — a park pace and a smart trot.

Usually bay (brownish) in color, the Hackney pony is sometimes black with white stockings and white head markings. They are a very alert pony, and usually stand twelve to fourteen hands high. (Hands is a way of measuring a horse's height from the highest point on the horse's shoulder to the ground. One hand is equal to four inches.) The Hackney's neck is long, but never thick, going into sloping shoulders and a sturdy body.

For showing in horse shows, the Hackney has two groups. The Cob-Tail and The Long Tail. The Long Tail pony is a cross between the Hackney and the Shetland. It has a long flowing mane and tail. The Cob-Tail has only a six inch (15 cm) tail that has been bobbed, and a tightly braided mane.

THE WELSH PONY

A long time ago, Welsh ponies pulled chariots in a war against the Romans. When the Romans invaded Wales, the people refused to surrender. Instead, they

This Welsh pony is used to pull a cart.

hid in the mountains. Their ponies went with them. During the winter, the ponies learned to paw through the snow to find grass and heather to eat. They uncovered food for the people's sheep, too. They became known as Welsh mountain ponies. Ceasar, the Roman leader, was so impressed by the strength of these small horses that he had some sent back to Rome.

The Welsh mountain pony is the most beautiful of

all pony breeds. It is sometimes called a miniature Arabian. It is a good riding pony, and also is good for pulling sleighs and wagons. The Welsh pony is used mostly by children. Sure-footed, it is often used for herding sheep. Like the Shetland, it has been used in the past for mining and carrying loads.

The Welsh pony can do many things. It is an outstanding hunter and jumper (these horses jump over obstacles). It can be ridden both English and Western style. (English and Western style riders use different kinds of saddles.) The Welsh pony is friendly and intelligent. Often, it is used in show rings for harness and roadster racing, and to pull carts.

The Welsh pony has bold eyes and a wide head. It's ears are small but alertly pointed and well shaped. It has a long neck, and strong muscles in its back and legs. Usually only twelve hands high, it can get as large as fourteen hands.

The coat of the Welsh pony is silky and soft. The mane, forelock and tail are full. Unlike the Hackney, the Welsh pony comes in many colors — brown, black, chestnut, bay, gray, roan, palomino, and dun. Sometimes there are white markings on the legs or head.

A quick learner and good worker, the Welsh pony also is gentle. It does not nip or kick. Another characteristic of this hardy breed is that it does not need horseshoes.

The Welsh pony is a gentle, quick learner, and a good worker.

17

THE ICELANDIC PONY

Around the year 875, the Viking Norsemen brought ponies to the island of Iceland. This breed of pony is still popular there today, but is rare in the United States. Only thirteen and one half hands high, the Icelandic pony is strong and powerful.

A popular sport in Iceland is trekking (cross-country riding.) The Icelandic pony is perfect for this. While the riders are camping for the night, the ponies graze or feed on grass. They can go twenty to forty miles (32-65 km) a day with no other feed. The ponies are also used for farm work such as pulling a plow.

The Icelandic is a fun pony to ride. It can walk, trot, canter, pace, and do a running-walk.

THE CONNEMARA PONY

In the middle 1500's, Spanish vessels, carrying horses, got shipwrecked off the coast of Ireland. The horses swam to shore and found a place to live. They mated with the horses already there, and the Connemara breed was begun. It is the best-known European breed. The Connemara is a sure-footed, mountain pony. It takes naturally to jumping and is safe and gentle, which makes it a good pony for hunters and children. It also is used for driving carts, and for sand racing.

The Connemara has a good sense of balance and is a good jumper. Strong bones and muscles in the hind quarters give it spring to jump barriers. Big sloping shoulders give them cushions for landing.

The Connemara is one of the tallest pony breeds.

THE NEW FOREST PONY

This pony comes from a place in England called New Forest. Once owned by William the Conqueror, who kept the New Forest for his hunting lands, the ponies that came from there soon were called New Forest ponies. They are gentle, big, short-legged and easy to ride. Intelligent, sturdy and easy to break, they make good polo ponies. They can hunt and jump and are easily harnessed.

The New Forest pony has been improved by use of Arabian and Thoroughbred sires. However, they are still not as popular as other European ponies.

PONIES OF THE AMERICAS (POA)

The Nez Perce Indians developed the Appaloosa horse. These Indians lived in the Palouse Country of Washington, Oregon, and Idaho. They captured wild spotted mustangs, and by careful breeding they came up with a strong, colorful, intelligent horse — the Appaloosa. With the coming of the white man, the Nez Perce were driven from their land. Settlers coming in wanted the Indian's grazing land. Eventually, the Nez Perce moved on, and the settlers got some of the horses as well as the land.

In 1955, a new pony was bred. It was called POA, or Pony of the Americas. This pony is a cross between an Appaloosa and a Shetland. It now is the most popular pony breed in the United States. The POA is a western-type pony, standing forty-six to fifty-four inches (118-138 cm) high. It is mostly Appaloosa in color. The POA serves in ways that the Shetland, Hackney and other types cannot. This tough little pony is good for cutting (dividing cattle), calf roping, trail-riding, hunting, and barrel racing.

The Pony of the Americas is registered by color.

The Pony of the Americas shows well in many events.

They have six basic markings: 1. Spotted blanket (spots on its back) 2. White blanket (almost all white back). 3. Leopard (spotted) 4. Snowflake (marks like snowflakes) 5. Frost (misty look) 6. Marble (swirling color). No single-colored pony can be called a true Pony of the Americas.

Other things that mark a pony of this breed include the following characteristics: white sclera (a covering over the eyeball) that makes it look like a human eye; a vertical stripe may be on one hoof or all four; mottled, or marbled skin often appears around the lips, muzzle, nostrils and eyes; sparse (thinly spred) mane and tail; lastly, "varnish" marks — these are small dark marks around the nose, eyes, mouth, and under the tail.

The Pony of the Americas is a good racer. It also is easily trained and shows well in pony shows.

The POA have distinct markings.

CHINCOTEAGUES
(Shing-co-teg)

This pony has a history similar to that of the Connemara. It is said that Spanish sailing vessels, on their way to Peru, were shipwrecked near what is now the state of Virginia. The ship's crew was drowned, but their ponies swam to the nearest land. This was the island of Assateague, off the cost of Virginia. Over the years, the ponies grew into herds of wild ponies. There was not much for them to eat except marsh grass, so they stayed a small size.

Members of the Volunteer Fire Department round up Chincoteague ponies each year.

Today, the herd is owned and supported by the Chincoteague Volunteer Fire Department. One day in July, every year, there is a Pony Penning Round-up. The firemen take off their helmets and put on their cowboy hats. Then they start the round-up. Ponies are herded into the water. They are made to swim from Assateague Island to Chincoteague Island. The ponies are guided by riders mounted on horses. Fifty ponies at a time are taken across the water, onto the land, and down the main street of Chincoteague. There they are put into a large corral and sold.

The ponies come ashore on Chincoteague Island, after swimming from Assateague Island.

23

The Walking pony is from the same family as the Tennessee Walking horses.

THE WALKING PONY

The Walking pony comes from the Tennessee Walking horse family. This pony has a good disposition. It doesn't nip, bite or kick. It has three gaits — walk, running-walk, and canter.

The Walking pony is solidly built. It has good shoulders, a barrel chest, a short back, and strong hind quarters. It's colors are black, sorrel, chestnut, roan, white, bay, brown, gray, palomino and spotted.

CROSSBRED PONY

The Crossbred is a large pony. It is used by children in fox hunting. This pony can jump walls and hedges. It is called a Crossbred pony because it is a cross between two breeds. It can be a cross between a Welsh pony and a Thoroughbred horse, or between two ponies, such as a Welsh and a Hackney. Crossbred ponies come in all colors.

The Crossbred is a large pony, which makes it a good jumper.

THE AMERICAN SADDLEBRED PONY

The American Saddlebred pony is a show pony. Wherever Saddle horses are popular, the Saddlebred ponies are too. This small pony came into being around the early 1900's. When demand for children's ponies increased, breeders began to breed the Saddle horse to ponies to get smaller stock.

The Saddlebred is an expensive pony. It takes a lot of training. But when trained, these ponies do what they are told and perform well.

They come in calico, bay, black, chestnut, sorrel, and palomino colors. They have the same face and leg markings as the Saddle horse. They are just miniatures of the larger horse.

THE MINIATURE OR MIDGET PONY

One of the most popular breeds is the Midget pony. Midget ponies, or miniatures, always are under thirty-two inches (82 cm) in height. Some even come as small as twenty inches (51 cm) — about the size of a medium-sized dog. Midget ponies are kept mostly as pets. They can be ridden, but only by small

Midget ponies have been used for a long time in Europe to pull small wagons.

children. In the 1850's, these ponies were popular in France. They were used for pulling small carriages.

Around 1850, miniature ponies were brought to America. A man named Walter McCoy took a liking to them and began a serious breeding program. His original herd of twelve miniature ponies soon multiplied into the largest miniature pony herd in the United States.

Today, many of the miniature ponies in the United States are descended from Mr. McCoy's herd. Other miniature ponies in this country originated in South America, on the Falabella Ranch. As a result, they are sometimes called Falabellas.

Miniature or midget ponies are about the size of a medium-size dog.

Midget ponies are well shaped. They look just like a very, very small horse. They are not dwarfs.

③
LEARNING ABOUT PONIES
IMPORTANT TERMS
TO KNOW

To learn about ponies it is helpful to know some terms associated with them. A pony is usually identified by color, height, sex and markings. Some breeds of ponies come only in certain colors.

"Appaloosa" ponies are usually dark, with a white "blanket" covered with polka dots across the rump. "Pinto" ponies are either piebald (white and black) or skewbald (white and any other color). They are also called spotted or paint.

A "buckskin" is a light yellow pony. "Dun" is a yellowish tan to mousey gray pony, with a black tail, mane, and legs and a black stripe down its back. An "albino," or white, pony has no color in its hair, skin or eyes.

"Gray" ponies turn almost white as they grow older. Some are born black and then change into a lighter color. A "sorrel" pony is yellow, gold or red, with a mane and tail of the same color. Much like the sorrel, the "palomino" pony is yellow-gold with a white mane and tail.

A "bay" pony has a black mane, tail, and legs, with a body color that varies from yellowish tan to dark brown. To be called "black," the pony must not have any other color on it. Sometimes a small white marking on its head or legs is permitted. If it has even a few brown hairs around the nostrils, it will be called a "brown" pony.

MARKINGS

Markings on ponies have special names. The term, black points, means the pony has a black mane, tail and legs, and often a dark stripe down its back.

Head markings are white. These markings are in different shapes. A "star" is a small white, star-shaped patch on the forehead. A "snip" is a white patch on the nose. A "stripe" is a long narrow stripe from the eyes to the nose. A "star and stripe" is a stripe down the forehead and the nose. A "blaze" is a wider stripe that almost reaches to each eye and goes down over the nose to the nostrils. And "bald" is almost a full white face.

Leg markings on a pony are called "socks" if they cover the ankle. "Half-stockings" are white markings half way to the knees. "Full-stockings" reach to the knees.

This pony has a small star on its forehead.

MORE TERMS
TO KNOW

The left side of the pony is called the near side. The right side is the off side. Riders should always mount on the near side.

Long ago, a horse began to be measured by hands. By turning the hand sideways and counting from the withers (where the mane begins at the shoulder) to the ground, a person could tell how tall a horse was. A hand is four inches. So eleven hands would be forty-four inches (112 cm). This method is still used

Always mount on the "near side," or left side, of the pony.

today for horses. However, ponies are usually measured in inches.

Movements of a pony's legs are called "gaits." The common gaits are walk, trot, canter and gallop (a fast canter).

Special terms describe how a pony looks or acts. A "typy" pony strongly shows particular traits of a breed. The "coarse" pony has bones that are too large and generally doesn't look the way it should. A "weedy" pony is narrow chested. A "rangy" pony is strong, with a long lean look. A "sound" pony is free of any blemish, injury or flaw.

The pony's "pedigree" tells the mother, father, grandparents, birthday, colors, markings, and name of breeder. Without papers that tell the pedigree, a pony's age can be told by looking at its teeth. Baby teeth are called "milk teeth." They are shed in the first year, and the pony acquires a "full mouth" of permanent teeth over a five year period. Permanent teeth have "cups" on them. After five to nine years of age the cups are worn down. When the cups are worn away by eating and grinding food, the pony is said to have a "smooth mouth." Later, a groove appears on the side of the teeth. This tells that the pony probably is at least ten years old.

SHOW PONIES

A halter pony represents what the breed should be. It is shown in a ring on a lead rope. The pony is judged on character and conformation (physical appearance), not on performance. In other words, the halter pony doesn't have to do anything but look good.

A harness pony is shown pulling a viceroy. These ponies must behave and look smart to get high points.

A roadster pony is harnessed to a sulky (a small cart in which a driver sits). The driver wears colorful "silks." Silks are the shirt and cap worn by the driver. They are in the horse owners colors and worn at all shows. This pony is judged on gait and form.

Hunter type ponies, like hunter horses, are good

The driver sits in a sulky as it's pulled by a Roadster pony.

jumpers. They are judged on style and speed when doing a series of jumps. They also are used to follow the hounds in fox hunting.

BEFORE OWNING
A PONY

Before owning a pony it is a good idea to know what its body parts are called. There are several reasons for this.

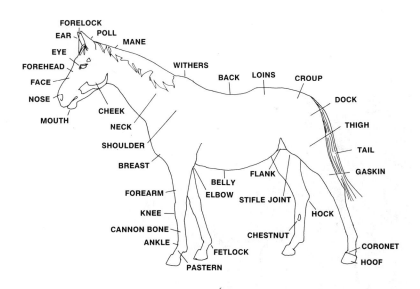

The parts of a pony.

When a pony is shown in the ring, the judge will ask the person showing the pony to name its parts.

It also is important to know the names of the pony's body parts because horse manuals list faults, or defects, by parts. Veterinarians, too, may expect pony owners to use the names of the parts of the animal when describing a health problem.

BUYING A PONY

Some people buy ponies at auctions. An auctioneer may say different things about the pony. "Serviceably sound" means the pony has no bad habits and its body, legs, eyes, and breathing are okay. "Legs go" means the pony is sound but may not look like much. "Chancy" is a winner in disguise. "A little bluish" means it only sees well out of one eye. The auctioneer tries to name things that the new owner should know. Then the bidding begins.

Another way to buy a pony is from a local riding school. The buyer can try out the pony before buying it. A pony can also be bought from a breeder at a pony show. There, it is easy to see the pony perform.

Some ponies may be bought from ads in horse magazines or newspapers. However, it is important to buy a pony only from a dealer or person with a good reputation.

THINGS TO LOOK FOR WHEN BUYING A PONY

The buyer should check if the pony can see by brushing a hand across each of the pony's eyes. If the pony blinks, it can see. If not, it may be blind. The pony's feet should be checked for injuries and defects such as cracks, splits, sores, or disease.

The buyer should handle the pony. If it acts calm, it's a good pony for children. If it's restless and fiery, it may be more suitable for another purpose. The buyer should choose a pony to fit the rider. If possible, the rider should bridle, saddle, and ride the pony before it is bought. If the buyer wants a pony for driving, it should be hitched up with a harness and cart and driven on a track.

The buyer should also check for good conformation. A short back is better for riding. A flat back won't hold a saddle. A well-rounded back is good. A pony with a long body is better used as a roadster or trotter (trotting ponies that pull carts). A pony with a narrow body is easier for children to sit astride.

The pony's legs and toes should be straight. If the toes turn in, the pony will swing out its hoofs when moving. Toes that are turned out will swing in when moving. This is not good because the pony may kick itself.

The wisest thing to do is to ask an expert for help in finding a good, healthy pony.

Shetland ponies have a heavy fur coat during the winter.

CARE OF THE PONY
SHELTER

Ponies are tougher than horses. They do not need a barn. A three-sided shed will do.

Ponies like to run, play and roll in the grass. They need a small pasture to be able to do this.

FEEDING

A pony needs about half the feed a horse does. Some ponies can live off grass in a pasture, but they

The food for these ponies is kept off the ground in a specially built bin.

like to be fed oats and corn too. One or two quarts (1.1-2.2 l) of grain two or three times a day should be enough. Besides grains and grass, ponies like hay.

Salt is an important part of a pony's diet. A salt block can be put out so the pony can lick at it.

Ponies also like apples, carrots, and sugar cubes. But too much sugar is not good for them. Neither is too much hay or grain.

Water should always be available, but never give water to a pony when it is hot or sweaty. First, walk it around and let it cool down. Then, wipe it dry and it can have all the water it needs.

GROOMING

Ponies need to be kept clean. They get dusty out in the pasture all day, so they must be brushed. Start just behind the ears on the left side, go down the neck and work back toward the tail. Then do the right side down the neck and back toward the tail. A currycomb should be used on the back, rubbing back and forth over the pony's coat. This loosens the dirt so it can be removed with a brush. Use the currycomb often to clean the brush.

A pony needs to be groomed from head to tail.

While grooming, it is a good idea to talk to the pony. Let it know what you are doing. Move slowly so you do not frighten it.

SHOEING

Horseshoes are not necessary on ponies. In fact, ponies shouldn't have shoes unless they are to be ridden on hard ground or streets. If you do decide to shoe your pony, the shoes should be reset every six to eight weeks. They are usually put on by a farrier, who is an expert in shoeing horses.

Stones sometimes get stuck in the pony's hoofs. These can be cleaned out with a hoof pick. But do it carefully. A pony has a soft V-shaped pad in the center of its hoof called the "frog." You must be careful when removing stones, so you don't hurt your pony.

SHOWING THE PONY

A well-groomed, well-mannered pony is ready for showing. There are several kinds of events in which the pony can be shown.

CONFORMATION AND SHOWMANSHIP

Although there is no way to change the ponies conformation, the person showing the pony can

41

point out it's best points through grooming and good manners.

In the show ring a pony is judged not only on its looks, but also on how well it obeys and poses. The showmanship of the rider is important, too. The judge will tell the rider what is expected. The judge may ask that the pony be led at a walk or trot. The judge may also want to look at the pony more closely. When the rider is asked to stop for this judging, the pony should be posed in one of two different ways. One way is a squared position, with an equal amount of weight on each of the pony's legs. The other is a stretched position, with front and hind legs moved slightly forward and backward respectively. However long it takes the judge to decide which pony is best, both rider and pony must remain alert.

EQUITATION

The saddle, or equitation, event may be divided into classes for beginning and advanced riders. To

Young riders walk their ponies during an equitation event.

enter, the rider must know how to walk the pony, to change gaits, to turn right and left, and to change directions. Other skills also are needed. The rider may be asked to show correct lead, to ride in a figure eight, or to ride bareback.

GYMKHANAS

Gymkhanas are organized games for ponies and riders. Because there are so many different kinds of

The egg and spoon race is a fun event.

games, it doesn't matter what the games are, as long as they show how well the rider and pony work together. Many gymkhanas are like games played in school — such as team relay races, musical chairs, break the balloon, potatoe races, and egg and spoon races.

JUMPING AND DRIVING

Two classes that require much training and practice are jumping and driving. There is more danger in these events because the rider has less control. The best way to learn how to jump and how to drive a cart are with a riding instructor.

TRICKS

Anyone watching a pony perform tricks in a circus or at a county fair might think it looks easy. An owner may try to teach a pony similar tricks at home. Probably the easiest trick is pickpocketing. In fact, the pony may try to do this on its own if it thinks there is a treat in the person's back pocket. If the pony discovers grain or an apple, it will pick the owner's pocket without being asked the next time.

Stealing a handkerchief is another easy trick if the pony thinks there's food waiting in it. First, grain should be sprinkled in the handkerchief and the pony should be allowed to eat from it. Then when

A natural-born pickpocket.

the handkerchief is returned to a pocket, the pony will steal it to see if there's a treat inside. There always should be a few bits of grain for the pony to find in the handkerchief.

Other tricks a pony will learn with a few lessons are mounting a pedestal, carrying a basket, and nodding it's head "yes" and "no." The pony can be taught to count by pawing with its hoofs.

Learning new tricks is just another part of the history of the animal that has survived for thousands of years. The pony has adjusted to life in the dinosaur era grasslands, on Viking ships, in coal mines, in the American west, and on farms. As a show animal and pet for today's owner or rider, the pony continues to show its adaptability.

GLOSSARY

ALBINO - A pure white pony with no color in skin or eyes.

APPALOOSA - A breed of pony with spotted marks.

BARREL - The body of a pony.

BAY - A brown pony with black mane, tail and legs.

BLAZE - A large white, wide mark on the pony's face from forehead to nose.

BREED - To bring forth offspring.

BRIDLE - The headgear used to control a pony. The main parts are the reins and bit.

CANTER - A fast trot, that becomes a gallop.

CONFORMATION - The physical outline of the pony's body.

CROSSBRED - A pony whose parents are purebred, but of different breeds — like Welsh and Hackney.

CURRY - To groom the coat, or hair, of a pony.

DAPPLED - Marked with spots across the rump.

EQUITATION - The art of riding.

FARRIER - One who puts horseshoes on ponies and horses.

FROG - "V" shaped pad on the sole of a pony's foot.

GAITS - Movements of a pony's legs — like walk, trot, canter.

GRADE PONY - A pony of mixed breeds with unknown ancestors.

GRAZE - To feed on grass in a pasture.

GYMKHANA - An organized game for a pony and rider.

HALTER - Leather or rope headpiece used for leading a pony around.

HAND - A hand is equal to four inches (10 cm), and is used to measure the height of a horse or pony.

LEAD - A rope that is snapped to the halter to lead a pony.

MANE - The long hair on top of a pony's neck.

PALOMINO - A golden-colored pony, with light or white mane and tail.

POINTS - The mane, tail, and lower legs of a pony.

REGISTRY - A place, or office, where lists of pony owners and ponies are kept. Each breed, or family of ponies keeps its own registry.

ROAN - A pony that has white hairs mixed with bay, sorrel, or black hairs.

RUMP - The heavy muscles of haunches and hips.

SULKY - A two-wheeled vehicle pulled by horses and ponies.

TROT - A medium-speed gait.

VETERINARIAN - A doctor trained to treat animals.

VICEROY - A four-wheeled vehicle, with one seat, for driving ponies.

WALK - A flat-footed, slow gait.

WITHERS - The highest point of the shoulder, where the mane begins.

THE HORSES

PASTURE TO PADDOCK

CRESTWOOD HOUSE